# ❧ DIRTIER ❧
# LITTLE LIMERICKS

# ❧ DIRTIER ❧
# LITTLE LIMERICKS

**Avenel Books**

**New York**

This edition is published by Avenel Books,
distributed by Crown Publishers, Inc.
h g f e d c
AVENEL 1981 EDITION

Manufactured in the United States of America

**Library of Congress Cataloging in Publication Data**
Main entry under title:

Dirtier little limericks.

  1. Limericks. 2. Bawdy poetry.
PN6231.L5E83   821'.08'08   81-3555
ISBN: 0-517-34803-9         AACR2

# FOREWORD

Over three hundred fifty years ago Ben Jonson wrote a poem that began, "Doing a filthy business is." Poor old Ben. If he were around today, he would not have such a negative outlook. "Doing" may still not be the cleanest activity in the world, but it is surely fun. A healthier, more realistic attitude toward "doing" (or perhaps the discovery of penicillin) has led to an increased enjoyment of this pastime.

But if it is more fun to do it, it is also more fun to be naughty about it. The writers of limericks are unsurpassed in this skill. They are so good at being naughty that—well, let's face it—they are downright dirty. Dirty as opposed to filthy, of course. If you were fortunate enough to pick up our first volume of frank five-liners, *Dirty Little Limericks,* you may find it hard to imagine that we dug up some dirtier ones. But here they are.

One is cheered that Edward Lear did not ruin a good literary genre and leave it stuck in the nursery. Although we know in our heart of hearts that the owl and the pussycat did more than dance by the light of the moon, such knowledge was never made public.

"Well," said the Wolf, "these three hundred fifty vivacious verses reveal things that Little Red Riding Hood's grandmother never dreamed of." Here you will be informed of Rosalina's ass, Scott and a twat, Miss Doves and her gloves, a wench who could do more than French, a man of Peru who had no one to screw, Jane with her cellophane—all these and more.

What other volume (besides our first) could give you a hearty har-har every five lines? What other volume could provide instruction for those unversed in the ways of the world?

Yes, it is all here. And if you are overcome with shock at first, we predict that you will soon give way to a chuckle, then to a gusty guffaw.

# ❧ DIRTIER ❧
# LITTLE LIMERICKS

There was a young lady of Exeter,
So pretty, that men craned their necks at her.
    One went so far
    As to wave from his car
The distinguishing mark of his sex at her.


There was a young fellow named Scott
Who took a girl out on his yacht—
    But too lazy to rape her
    He made darts of brown paper,
Which he languidly tossed at her twat.


"I insist." "It's no good." "But you must."
"Think of me." "Think of masculine lust."
    "What a bore." "Why, you whore!
    You promised before."
"And the mink! Is that got through trust?"

An ancient but jolly old bloke
Once picked up a girl for a poke;
    First took down her pants,
    Fucked her into a trance,
Then shit in her shoe for a joke.

❧

There was a young lady named Dowd
Whom a young fellow groped in the crowd.
    But the thing that most vexed her
    Was that when he stood next her
He said, "How's your cunt?" right out loud.

❧

There was a young student of Trinity
Who shattered his sister's virginity.
    He buggered his brother,
    Had twins by his mother,
And took double honours in Divinity.

❧

The gay young Duke of Buckingham
Stood on the bridge at Rockingham
    Watching the stunts
    Of the cunts and the punts
And the tricks of the pricks that were fucking 'em.

Said Oscar McDingle O'Figgle,
With an almost hysterical giggle,
   "Last night I was sick
   With delight when my prick
Felt dear Alfred's delicious ass wriggle!"


A vice both obscure and unsavory
Kept the Bishop of Chester in slavery:
   Midst terrible howls
   He deflowered young owls
In his crypt fitted out as an aviary.


A hermit who had an oasis
Thought it the best of all places:
   He could pray and be calm
   'Neath a pleasant date-palm,
While the lice on his ballocks ran races.


"Fuck me quick, fuck me deep, fuck me oft
In the bog, in the bath, in the loft,
   Up my ass, up my quim,
   Knees, armpits, lip rim
With your prick, but *please*, nothing soft."

A preposterous King of Siam
Said, "For women I don't care a damn.
   But a fat-bottomed boy
   Is my pride and my joy—
They call me a bugger: I am!"


There are three ladies of Huxham,
And whenever we meets 'em we fucks 'em.
   When that game grows stale
   We sits on a rail,
Pulls out our pricks, and they sucks 'em.


Then up spake the Bey of Algiers,
"I've been knocking around for long years,
   And my language is blunt:
   A cunt IS a cunt
And fucking IS fucking"—(loud cheers).


Hearing this, mewed the young King of Spain,
"To fuck and to bugger is shame.
   But it's not *infra dig*.
   To occasionally frig—
So I do it again and again."

When Titian was mixing rose madder,
His model was poised on a ladder.
    "Your position," said Titian,
    "Inspires coition."
So he nipped up the ladder and 'ad 'er.


❧

An organist playing in York
Had a prick that could hold a small fork.
    And between obligatos
    He'd much at tomatoes,
And keep up his strength while at work.


❧

It always delights me at Hanks
To walk up the old river banks.
    One time in the grass
    I stepped on an ass,
And heard a young girl murmur, "Thanks!"


❧

"Far dearer to me than my treasure,"
The heiress declared, "is my leisure.
    For then I can screw
    The whole Harvard crew—
They're slow, but that lengthens the pleasure."

There was a young man from the Coast
Who had an affair with a ghost.
    At the height of the orgasm
    Said the pallid phantasm,
"I think I can feel it—almost!"


There was a young lady from Kew
Who filled her vagina with glue.
    She said with a grin,
    "If they pay to get in,
They'll pay to get out of it too."


Here's to it, and through it, and to it again,
To suck it, and screw it, and screw it again!
    So in with it, out with it,
    Lord work his will with it!
Never a day we don't do it again!


There was a debauched little wench
Whom nothing could ever make blench.
    She admitted men's poles
    At all possible holes,
And she'd bugger, fuck, jerk off, and french.

There was a young man of Coblenz
Whose ballocks were simply immense:
   It took forty-four draymen,
   A priest and three laymen
To carry them thither and thence.

There was a young maid named Clottery
Who was having a fuck on a rockery.
   She said, "Listen chum,
   You've come on my bum!
This isn't a fuck, it's a mockery."

A sweet young strip-dancer named Jane
Wore five inches of thin cellophane.
   When asked why she wore it
   She said, "I abhor it,
But my cunt juice would spatter like rain."

An agreeable girl named Miss Doves
Likes to jack off the young men she loves.
   She will use her bare fist
   If the fellows insist
But she really prefers to wear gloves.

The Rajah of Afghanistan
Imported a Birmingham can,
    Which he set as a throne
    On a great Buddha stone—
But he crapped out-of-doors like a man.


ও

A scandal involving an oyster
Sent the Countess of Clewes to a cloister,
    She preferred it in bed
    To the Count, so she said,
Being longer, and stronger, and moister.


ও

A lady on climbing Mount Shasta
Complained as the mountain grew vaster,
    That it wasn't the climb
    Nor the dirt and the grime,
But the ice on her ass that harassed her.


ও

When a woman in strapless attire
Found her breasts working higher and higher,
    A guest, with great feeling,
    Exclaimed, "How appealing!
Do you mind if I piss in the fire?"

There was a young Angel called Cary
Who kissed, stroked and fucked Virgin Mary.
    And Christ was so bored
    At seeing Mom whored
That he set Himself up as a fairy.

❦

There was a young girl of Devon
Who was raped in the garden by seven
    High Anglican Priests—
    The lascivious beasts—
Of such is the kingdom of Heaven.

❦

There was a young man of Bengal
Who went to a fancy dress ball.
    He was draped like a tree
    Having failed to foresee
Being pissed on by dogs, cats, and all.

❦

A maiden who lived in Virginny
Had a cunt that could bark, neigh and whinny.
    The hunting set chased her,
    Fucked, buggered, then dropped her
For the pitch of her organ went tinny.

" 'Tis my custom," said dear Lady Norris,
"To beg lifts from the drivers of lorries.
    When they get out to piss
    I see things that I miss
At the wheel of my two-seater Morris."


A mediaeval recluse named Sissions
Was alarmed by his nightly emissions.
    His cell-mate, a sod,
    Said, "Leave it to God."
And taught him some nifty positions.


In the city of Paris are wives
Who, when not scratching their hives,
    Are waiting for tourists
    Who might act as purists
And give them the ride of their lives.


There was a young artist named Frentzel
Whose tool was as sharp as a pencil.
    He pricked through an actress,
    The sheet and the mattress,
And busted the bedroom utensil.

All the lady-apes ran from King Kong
For his dong was unspeakably long.
    But a friendly giraffe
    Quaffed his yard and a half,
And ecstatically burst into song.

&#x2767;

The prior of Dunstan St. Just,
Consumed with erotical lust,
    Raped the bishop's prize fowls,
    Buggered four startled owls
And a little green lizard, that bust.

&#x2767;

"In my salad days," said Lady Bierley,
"I took my cocks fairly and squarely.
    But now when they come
    They go right up my bum—
And that only happens but rarely."

&#x2767;

The Marquesa de Excusador
Used to pee on the drawing-room floor,
    For the can was so cold
    And when one grows old
To be much alone is a bore.

"It's been a very full day,"
Yawned Lady Mary McDougle McKay.
   "Three cherry tarts,
   At least twenty farts,
Two shits and a bloody fine lay."


An elderly pervert in Nice
Who was long past wanting a piece
   Would jack-off his hogs,
   His cows and his dogs,
Till his parrot called in the police.


"Great God!" wailed Peter McGuff,
What the devil is all of this stuff!
   She twiddles my prick,
   Gets it stiff as a stick,
And denies me the use of her muff."


There was a young parson named Binns
Who talked about women and things.
   But his secret desire
   Was a boy in the choir
With a bottom like jelly on springs.

There was a young Scot of Delray
Who buggered his father one day,
    Saying, "I like it rather
    To stuff it up Father;
He's clean—and there's nothing to pay."


There was an old man of Dundee,
Who came home as drunk as could be.
    He wound up the clock
    With the end of his cock,
And buggered his wife with the key.


There was an old critic named West
Whose penis came up to his chest.
    He said, "I declare,
    I have no pubic hair."
So he covered his nuts with his vest.


The nephew of one of the czars
Used to suck off Rasputin at Yars,
    'Til the peasants revolted,
    The royal family bolted—
Now they're under the sickle and stars.

There was a young lady named Alice
Who was having a piss in a chalice.
   "What a stunt," said a monk,
   "To twiddle your cunt,
Not through need but through Protestant malice."


❧


There was a young student named Howells
Shot his sperm o'er a young coed's bowels.
   He said, "I regret
   That I've made you so wet—
And I fear I am quite out of towels."


❧


There was an old man who could piss
Through a ring—and what's more, never miss.
   Marksmen queued up to cheer,
   Bought him beer after beer,
And swore oaths on his urinal hiss.


❧


There was a young man of high station
Who was found by a pious relation
   Making love in a ditch
   To—I won't say a bitch—
But a woman of *no* reputation.

A broken-down harlot named Tupps
Was heard to confess in her cups:
    "The height of my folly
    Was fucking a collie–
But I got a nice price for the pups."

A passionate red-headed girl,
When you kissed her, her senses would whirl,
    And her twat would get wet
    And would wiggle and fret,
And her cunt-lips would curl and unfurl.

There was a young man from Lynn
Whose cock was the size of a pin.
    Said his girl with a laugh
    As she fondled his staff,
"This won't be much of a sin."

To his bride a young bridegroom said, "Pish!
Your cunt is as big as a dish!"
    She replied, "Why, you fool,
    With your limp little tool
It's like driving a nail with a fish!"

There was a young fellow named Brewster
Who said to his wife as he goosed her,
    "It used to be grand
    But just look at my hand!
You ain't wiping as clean as you used to."

❧

There was a young girl named McCall
Whose cunt was exceedingly small,
    But the size of her anus
    Was something quite heinous—
It could hold seven pricks and one ball.

❧

A cretin who lived in an attic
Was fallaciously rated as static;
    But how little they knew—
    His knob was not blue—
But hoary and necrophilatic.

❧

There was a young girl of Dundee
Who was raped by an ape in a tree.
    The result was most horrid—
    All ass and no forehead,
Three balls and a purple goatee.

Thus spake I AM THAT I AM:
"For the Virgin I don't give a damn,
    What pleases me most
    Is to bugger the Ghost,
And then be sucked off by the Lamb."

❧

When a lecherous curate at Leeds
Was discovered, one day, in the weeds
    Astride a young nun,
    He said, "Christ, this is fun!
Far better than telling one's beads!"

❧

There was a young lady of Crewe
Whose cherry a chap had got through—
    Which she told to her mother
    Who fixed her another
Out of rubber and red ink and glue.

❧

There was a young dancer, Priscilla,
Who flavored her cunt with vanilla.
    The taste was so fine,
    Men and beasts stood in line,
Including a stud armadilla.

The priest, a cocksucker named Sheen,
Is delighted his sins are not seen.
   "Though God sees through walls,"
   Says Monsignor, "–Oh, balls!
This God stuff is simply a screen."


There was a young girl in Alsace
Who was having her first piece of ass.
   "Oh, darling you'll kill me!
   Oh, dearest, you thrill me
Like Father John's thumb after mass!"


A modern young lady named Hall
Went out to a birth-controll ball.
   She was loaded with pessaries
   And other accessories,
But no one approached her at all.


A handsome young monk in a wood
Told a girl she should cling to the good.
   She obeyed him, and gladly;
   He repulsed her, but sadly:
"My dear, you have misunderstood."

There was a young man of St. Johns
Who wanted to bugger the swans.
　　"Oh no," said the porter,
　　"You bugger my daughter,
Them swans is reserved for the Dons."

　　　　　　ح

There was a young man from Axminster
Whose designs were quite base and quite sinister.
　　His lifelong ambition
　　Was anal coition
With the wife of the French foreign minister.

　　　　　　ح

A team playing baseball in Dallas
Called the umpire a shit out of malice.
　　While this worthy had fits,
　　The team made eight hits
And a girl in the bleachers named Alice.

　　　　　　ح

"For the tenth time, dull Daphnis," said Chloe,
"You have told me my bosom is snowy;
　　You have made much fine verse on
　　Each part of my person,
Now *do* something— there's a good boy!"

There was a young girl of Detroit
Who at fucking was very adroit:
    She could squeeze her vagina
    To a pin-point, or finer,
Or open it out like a quoit.

And she had a friend named Durand
Whose cock could contract or expand.
    He could diddle a midge
    Or the arch of a bridge–
Their performance together was grand!

❧

There was a young lady named Hall
Wore a newspaper dress to a ball.
    The dress caught on fire
    And burned her entire
Front page, sporting section, and all.

❧

A disgusting young man named McGill
Made his neighbors exceedingly ill
    When they learned of his habits
    Involving white rabbits
And a bird with a flexible bill.

There was a young fellow from Leeds
Who swallowed a package of seeds.
   Great tufts of grass
   Sprouted out of his ass
And his balls were all covered with weeds.

❧

There was a young girl whose divinity
Preserved her in perfect virginity.
   Till a candle, her nemesis,
   Caused parthenogenesis—
Now she thinks herself one of the Trinity.

❧

In the reign of King George the Third,
The fashionable fuck was a bird:
   The hole of a sparrow
   Was dry, pink and narrow,
And was oiled with hummingbirds' turd.

❧

There was a young lady named Nelly
Whose tits could be joggled like jelly.
   They could tickle her twat,
   Or be tied in a knot,
And could even swat flies on her belly.

"The testes are cooler outside,"
Said the doc to the curious bride.
   "For the semen must not
   Get too fucking hot,
And the bag fans your bum on the ride."


ᒚ


There was an old parson of Lundy,
Fell asleep in his vestry on Sunday.
   He awoke with a scream:
   "What, another wet dream!
That's what comes from not frigging since Monday."


ᒚ


Said Edna St. Vincent Millay
As she lay in the hay all asplay,
   "If you can make wine
   From these grapes, I opine,
We'll stay in this barn until May."


ᒚ


A chap down in Oklahoma
Had a cock that could sing *La Paloma*,
   But the sweetness of pitch
   Couldn't put off the hitch
Of impotence, size and aroma.

The grand-niece of Madame Du Barry
Suspected her son was a fairy.
    "It's peculiar," said she,
    "But he sits down to pee,
And stands when I bathe the canary."


ॐ


A gentleman living in Fife
Made love to the corpse of his wife.
    "How could I know, Judge?
    She was cold, did not budge—
Just the same as she'd acted in life."


ॐ


While pissing on deck, an old boatswain
Fell asleep, and his pisser got frozen.
    It snapped at the shank
    It fell off and sank
In the sea—'twas his own fault for dozin'!


ॐ


When a girl, young Elizabeth Barrett
Was found by her Ma in a garret,
    She had shoved up a diamond
    As far as her hymen,
And was ramming it home with a carrot.

There was a young fellow of Mayence
Who fucked his own ass in defiance
   Not only of habit
   And morals but—damn it!—
Most of the known laws of science.

&#10547;

There was a young lady of Cheam
Who crept into the vestry unseen.
   She pulled down her knickers,
   Likewise the vicar's
And said, "How about it, old bean?"

&#10547;

"At a seance," said a young man named Post,
"I was being sucked off by a ghost;
   Someone switched on the lights
   And there in gauze tights,
On his knees, was Tobias mine host."

&#10547;

In his garden remarked Lord Larkeeling:
"A fig for your digging and weeding.
   I like watching birds
   While they're dropping their turds,
And spying on guinea pigs breeding."

There was a young girl of Kilkenny
On whose genital parts there were many
    Venereal growths—
    The result of wild oats
Sown there by a fellow named Benny.

&#10087;

The modern cinematic emporium
Is not just a super-sensorium
    But a highly effectual
    Heterosexual
Mutual masturbatorium.

&#10087;

When Brother John wanted a screw
He would stuff a fat cat in a shoe,
    Pull up his cassock
    And kneel on a hassock
While doing his damnedest to mew.

&#10087;

"It's dull in Duluth, Minnesota,
Of spirit there's not an iota—"
    Complained Alice to Joe
    Who tried not to show
That he yawned in her snatch as he blowed her.

The Shah of the Empire of Persia
Lay for days in a sexual merger.
　　When the nautch asked the Shah,
　　"Won't you ever withdraw?"
He replied with a yawn, "It's inertia."


ح


There was a young curate of Eltham
Who wouldn't fuck girls, but he felt 'em.
　　In lanes he would linger
　　And play at stick-finger,
And scream with delight when he smelt 'em.


ح


A disciple of symbolist Jung,
Asked his wife, "May I bugger your bung?"
　　And was so much annoyed
　　When he found she read Freud,
He went out in the yard and ate dung.


ح


Said the Duchess of Danzer at tea,
"Young man, do you fart when you pee?"
　　I replied with some wit,
　　"Do you belch when you shit?"
I think that was one up for me.

A marine being sent to Hong Kong
Got a doctor to alter his dong.
    He sailed off with a tool
    Flat and thin as a rule—
When he got there he found he was wrong.

&#42;

A finicky young whippersnapper
Had ways so revoltingly dapper
    That a young lady's quim
    Didn't interest him
If it hadn't a cellophane wrapper.

&#42;

"Well, I took your advice," said McKnopp,
"And told the wife to get up on top.
    She bounced about a bit,
    Didn't quite get the hang of it,
And the kids, much amused, made us stop."

&#42;

There was a young lady of Rheims
Who amazingly pissed four streams.
    A friend poked around
    And a fly-button found
Wedged tightly in one of her seams.

A geneticist living in Delft,
Scientifically played with himself;
   When he was done
   He labeled it: *Son,*
And filed him away on the shelf.

❧

While fucking one night, Dr. Zuck
In his ears got his wife's nipples stuck.
   With his thumb up her bum,
   He could hear himself come—
This inventing the Telephone Fuck.

❧

There was a young fellow named Howell
Who buggered himself with a trowel.
   The triangular shape
   Was conducive to rape,
And was easily cleaned with a towel.

❧

There was a young man from Port Said
Who fell down a shit-house and died.
   His unfortunate mother,
   She fell down another;
And now they're interred side by side.

A gentle old Dame they called Muir
Had a mind so delightfully pure
    That she fainted away
    At a friend's house one day
When she saw some canary manure.


&#x2767;


I dined with Lord Hughy Fitz-Bluing
Who said "Do you squirm when you're screwing?"
    I replied "Simple shagging
    Without any wagging
Is only for screwing canoeing."


&#x2767;


There was a young man in Woods Hole
Who had an affair with a mole.
    Though a bit of a nancy
    He *did like* to fancy
Himself in the dominant role.


&#x2767;


"Remind me, dear," said Sir Keith,
"As soon as I've brushed my teeth,
    To take down this glass
    And examine my ass
From behind—and of course from beneath."

A pious young lady named Finnegan
Would caution her friend, "Well, you're in again;
   So time it aright,
   Make it last through the night,
For I certainly don't want to sin again!"

&#x25b6;

A circus performer named Ditts
Was subject to passionate fits,
   But his pleasure in life
   Was to suck off his wife
As he swung by his knees from her tits.

&#x25b6;

Young girls who frequent picture-palaces
Are amused at the vogue of analysis,
   And giggle that Freud
   Should be less than annoyed
While they tickle contemporary phalluses.

&#x25b6;

A musical student from Sparta
Was a truly magnificent farter:
   On the strength of one bean
   He'd fart "God Save the Queen,"
And Beethoven's "Moonlight Sonata."

An avant-garde bard named McNamiter
Had a tool of enormous diameter.
    But it wasn't the size
    Brought tears to her eyes.
'Twas the rhythm—dactylic hexameter!

&

There was a young girl of Peru
Who had nothing whatever to do,
    So she sat on the stairs
    And counted cunt hairs—
Four thousand, three hundred, and two.

&

There was a young fellow of Eversham
Wrote a treatise on cunts and on sucking them.
    But a lady from Wales
    Took the wind from his sails
With an essay on ass-holes and fucking them.

&

"Now listen, young girl," said McPhett,
"You tell me your cunt is all wet.
    Yet when I shove, you squirm,
    Waste my boiling hot sperm—
You don't want to fuck, only sweat!"

Dr. John Donne, a Dean to St. Paul,
Grew old, and his prick rather small.
　　Though he buggered a bug
　　At the edge of a rug,
The insect scarce felt it at all.


❧


There once was a sailor from Wales,
An expert at pissing in gales.
　　He could piss in a jar
　　From the top-gallant spar
Without even wetting sails.


❧


Cleopatra, while helping to pump,
Ground out such a furious bump
　　That Antony's dick
　　Snapped off like a stick
And left him to pump with the stump.


❧


There once was a curate named Swope
Who wanted to bugger the Pope—
　　To destroy the division
　　Twixt his lust and religion
And, on the side, get an Archbishop's cope.

There was a young fellow named Lock
Who was born with a two-headed cock.
　　When he'd fondle the thing
　　It would rise up and sing
An antiphonal chorus by Bach.


But whether these two ever met
Has not been recorded as yet—
　　Still, it would be diverting
　　To see him inserting
His whang while it sang a duet!


❧


In spite of a wasting disease
O'Reilly went down on his knees
　　Before altars of gods,
　　Whores, boys, and small dogs—
And all this for very small fees.


❧


A piano composer named Liszt
Played with one hand while he pissed.
　　But as he grew older
　　His technique grew bolder,
And in concert jacked off with his fist.

There lives a young girl in New York
Who is cautious from fear of the stork.
   You will find she is taped
   To prevent being raped,
And her ass-hole is plugged with a cork.

·

In bed Dr. Oscar McPugh
Spoke of Spengler—and ate crackers too.
   His wife said, "Oh, stuff
   That philosophy guff
Up your ass, dear, and throw me a screw!"

·

A Sunday-School student in Mass.
Soon rose to the head of the class,
   By reciting quite bright
   And sleeping at night
With his tongue up the minister's ass.

·

While out on a picnic, McFee
Was stung on the balls by a bee.
   He made oodles of money
   By oozing pure honey
Every time he attempted to pee.

There was a young man of Bombay
Who fashioned a cunt out of clay.
    The heat of his prick
    Turned the damned thing to brick
And wore all his foreskin away.

❧

To succeed in the brothels at Derna
One always begins as a learner.
    Indentured at six
    As a greaser of pricks,
One may rise to be fitter and turner.

❧

There was a young lady whose joys
Were achieved with incomparable poise.
    She could have an orgasm
    With never a spasm—
She could fart without making a noise.

❧

When Theocritus guarded his flock
He piped in the shade of a rock.
    It is said that his Muse
    Was one of the ewes
With a bum like a pink hollyhock.

There once was a son-of-a-bitch,
Neither clever, nor handsome, nor rich,
   Yet the girls he would dazzle,
   And fuck to a frazzle,
And then *ditch* them, the son-of-a-bitch!


&#x2767;


There was a young fellow named Blaine,
And he screwed some disgusting old jane.
   She was ugly and smelly,
   With an awful pot-belly,
But . . . well, they were caught in the rain.


&#x2767;


A middle-aged codger named Bruin
Found his love life completely a-ruin,
   For he flirted with flirts
   Wearing pants and no skirts,
And he never got in for no screwin'.


&#x2767;


There was a young man from Calcutta
Who was heard in his beard to mutter,
   "If her Bartholin glands
   Don't respond to my hands,
I'm afraid I shall have to use butter."

There once was a kiddie named Carr
Caught a man on top of his mar.
   As he saw him stick 'er,
   He said with a snicker,
"You do it much faster than par."


&#x2767;


There once was a gouty old colonel
Who grew glum when the weather grew vernal,
   And he cried in his tiffin
   For his prick wouldn't stiffen,
And the *size* of the thing was infernal.


&#x2767;


A lonely young lad of Eton
Used always to sleep with the heat on,
   Till he ran into a lass
   Who showed him her ass—
Now they sleep with only a sheet on.


&#x2767;


A reckless young lady of France
Had no qualms about taking a chance,
   But she thought it was crude
   To get screwed in the nude,
So she always went home with damp pants.

Have you heard of knock-kneed Samuel McGuzzum
Who married Samantha, his bow-legged cousin?
    Some people say
    Love finds a way,
But for Sam and Samantha it doesn'.


❧


There was a young lady named May
Who strolled in a park by the way,
    And she met a young man
    Who fucked her and ran—
Now she goes to the park every day.


❧


There once was a Swede in Minneapolis,
Discovered his sex life was hapless:
    The more he would screw
    The more he'd want *to*,
And he feared he would soon be quite sapless.


❧


There was a young dolly named Molly
Who thought that to frig was folly.
    Said she, "You pee-pee
    Means nothing to me,
But I'll do it just to be jolly."

"I once knew a harlot named Lou—
And a versatile girl she was, too.
   After ten years of whoredom
   She perished of boredom
When she married a jackass like you!"


There was a young lady of Gloucester
Whose friends they thought they had lost her,
   Till they found on the grass
   The marks of her arse,
And the knees of the man who had crossed her.


Winter is here with his grouch,
The time when you sneeze and slouch.
   You can't take you women
   Canoein' or swimmin',
But a lot can be done on a couch.


A worn-out young husband named Lehr
Heard daily his wife's plaintive prayer:
   "Slip on a sheath, quick,
   Then slip your big dick
Between these lips covered with hair."

There was a young man of Ostend
Who let a girl play with his end.
   She took hold of Rover,
   And felt it all over,
And it did what she didn't intend.

&#x2767;

There was a young man of Ostend
Whose wife caught him fucking her friend.
   "It's no use, my duck,
   Interrupting your fuck,
For I'm damned if I draw till I spend."

&#x2767;

A newly-wed man of Peru
Found himself in a terrible stew:
   His wife was in bed
   Much deader than dead,
And so he had no one to screw.

&#x2767;

His wife had a nice little cunt:
It was hairy, and soft, and in front,
   And with this she would fuck him,
   Though sometimes she'd suck him—
A charming, if commonplace, stunt.

I could hear the dull buzz of the bee
As he sunk his grub hooks into me.
   Her ass it was fine
   But you should have seen mine
In the shade of the old apple tree.


❧


There was a young lady named Twiss
Who said she thought fucking a bliss,
   For it tickled her bum
   And caused her to come
While comfortably lying like this.


❧


There was a young lady named Blount
Who had a rectangular cunt.
   She learned for diversion
   Posterior perversion,
Since no one could fit her in front.


❧


There was a young lady named Brent
With a cunt of enormous extent,
   And so deep and so wide,
   The acoustics inside
Were so good you could hear when you spent.

There once was a Queen of Bulgaria
Whose bush had grown hairier and hairier,
   Till a Prince from Peru
   Who came up for a screw
Had to hunt for her cunt with a terrier.

&#10087;

I met a young man in Chungking
Who had a very long thing—
   But you'll guess my surprise
   When I found that its size
Just measured a third-finger ring!

&#10087;

There once was a girl from Cornell
Whose teats were shaped like a bell.
   When you touched them they shrunk,
   Except when she was drunk,
And then they got bigger than hell.

&#10087;

There was a young lady whose cunt
Could accommodate a small punt.
   Her mother said, "Annie,
   It matches your fanny,
Which never was that of a runt."

There was a young man from East Wubley
Whose cock was bifurcated doubly.
    Each quadruplicate shaft
    Had two balls hanging aft,
And the general effect was quite lovely.

❧

There was a young fellow of Greenwich
Whose balls were all covered with spinach.
    He had such a tool
    It was wound on a spool,
And he reeled it out inich by inich.

But this tale has an unhappy finich,
For due to the sand in the spinach
    His ballocks grew rough
    And wrecked his wife's muff,
And scratched up her thatch in the scrimmage.

❧

There was a young fellow of Harrow
Whose john was the size of a marrow.
    He said to his tart,
    "How's this for a start?
My balls are outside in a barrow."

There was a young girl named Heather
Whose twitcher was made out of leather.
    She made a queer noise,
    Which attracted the boys,
By flapping the edges together.

❧

Oh, pity the Duchess of Kent!
Her cunt is so dreadfully bent,
    The poor wench doth stammer,
    "I need a sledgehammer
To pound a man into my vent."

❧

A contortionist hailing from Lynch
Used to rent out his tool by the inch.
    A foot cost a quid—
    He could and he did
Stretch it to three in a pinch.

❧

A farmer I know named O'Doole
Has a long and incredible tool.
    He can used it to plow,
    Or to diddle a cow,
Or just as a cue-stick at pool.

When I was a baby, my penis
Was as white as the buttocks of Venus.
   But now 'tis as red
   As her nipples instead—
All because of the feminine genus!

❧

A very odd pair are the Pitts:
His balls are as large as her tits,
   Her tits are as large
   As an invasion barge—
Neither knows how the other cohabits.

❧

A beautiful lady named Psyche
Is loved by a fellow named Ikey.
   One thing about Ike
   The lady can't like
Is his prick, which is dreadfully spikey.

❧

There was a young harlot named Schwartz
Whose cock-pit was studded with warts,
   And they tickled so nice
   She drew a high price
From the studs at the summer resorts.

There was a young lady named Astor
Who never let any get past her.
   She finally got plenty
   By stopping at twenty,
Which certainly ought to last her.


ั.


There was an old man of Cajon
Who never could get a good bone.
   With the aid of a gland
   It grew simply grand;
Now his wife cannot leave it alone.


ั.


There once was a lady named Carter,
Fell in love with a virile young Tartar.
   She stripped off his pants,
   At his prick quickly glanced,
And cried: "For that I'll be a martyr!"


ั.


There was a young man with a fiddle
Who asked of his girl, "Do you diddle?"
   She replied, "Yes, I do,
   But prefer to with two—
It's twice as much fun in the middle."

There was a young fellow named Fletcher,
Was reputed an infamous lecher.
    When he'd take on a whore
    She'd need a rebore,
And they'd carry him out on a stretcher.


۶


I know of a fortunate Hindu
Who is sought in the towns that he's been to
    By the ladies he knows,
    Who are thrilled to the toes
By the tricks he can make his foreskin do.


۶


There was a young miss from Johore
Who'd lie on a mat on the floor;
    In a manner uncanny
    She'd wobble her fanny,
And drain your nuts dry to the core.


۶


There was a young lady named Mable
Who liked to sprawl out on the table,
    Then cry to her man,
    "Stuff in all you can—
Get your ballocks in, too, if you're able."

There was a young lady named Nance
Who learned about fucking in France,
    And when you'd insert it
    She'd squeeze till she hurt it,
And shoved it right back in your pants.


ॐ


There was a young girl named O'Clare
Whose body was covered with hair.
    It was really quite fun
    To probe with one's gun,
For her quimmy might be anywhere.


ॐ


While spending the winter at Pau
Lady Pamela forgot to say "No."
    So the head-porter made her
    The second-cook laid her;
The waiters were all hanging low.


ॐ


'Tis said that the Emperor Titius
Had a penchant for pleasantries vicious.
    He took two of his nieces
    And fucked them to pieces,
And said it was simply delicious.

There was a young man from Toledo
Who was cursed with excessive libido.
   To fuck and to screw,
   And to fornicate too,
Were the three major points of his credo.


A virile young man of Touraine.
Had vesicles no one could drain.
   With an unbroken flow
   Thrice the course he would go,
Then roll over and start in again.


A young man with a passion quite vast
Used to talk about making it last,
   Till one day he discovered
   His sister uncovered,
And now he fucks often—and fast.


There was a young fellow from Wark
Who, when he screws, has to bark.
   His wife is a bitch
   With a terrible itch,
So the town never sleeps after dark.

There was a young girl of Samoa
Who plugged up her cunt with a boa.
   This strange contraceptive
   Was very deceptive
To all but the spermatozoa.

<br>

There's an over-sexed lady named Whyte
Who insists on a dozen a night.
   A fellow named Cheddar
   Had the brashness to wed her—
His chance of survival is slight.

<br>

Said a man to a maid of Ashanti,
"Can one sniff of your twitchet, or can't he?"
   Said she with a grin,
   "Sure, shove your nose in!
But *presto,* please—not too *andante.*"

<br>

There was a young lass of Blackheath
Who frigged an old man with her teeth.
   She complained that he stunk
   Not so much from the spunk,
But his arsehole was just underneath.

A girl with a sebaceous cyst
Always came when her asshole was kissed.
 Her lover was gratified
 That she was so satisfied,
But regretted the fun that he missed.


&#818;

There once was a maid in Duluth,
A striver and seeker of truth.
 This pretty wench
 Was adept at French,
And said all else was uncouth.


&#818;

There was a young lady named Hix
Who was fond of sucking big pricks.
 One fellow she took
 Was a doctor named Snook,
Now *he's* in a hell of a fix.


&#818;

There was a young lady named Grace
Who took all she could in her face,
 But an adequate lad
 Gave her all that he had,
And blew tonsils all over the place.

The priests at the temple of Isis
Used to offer up amber and spices,
    Then back of the shrine
    They would play 69
And other unmentionable vices.

᭞

A Roman of old named Horatio
Was fond of a form of fellatio.
    He kept accurate track
    Of the boys he'd attack,
And called it his cock-sucking ratio.

᭞

There was an old maid from Luck
Who took it into her head to fuck.
    She was about to resign
    Till she hung out a sign:
"Come in, I've decided to suck."

᭞

There was a young bounder named Link
Who possessed a very tart dink.
    To sweeten it some
    He steeped it in rum,
And he's driven the ladies to drink.

Said the priest to Miss Bridget McLennin,
"Sure, a kiss of your twat isn't sinnin'."
    And he stuck to this story
    Till he tasted the gory
And menstruous state she was then in.

❧

A socialite out on Nantucket
Had a twat that was wide as a bucket.
    She proclaimed, "If it's clean
    I will take it between—
If it's rotten I'd far better suck it."

❧

An old doctor who lacked protoplasm
Tried to give his young wife an orgasm,
    But his tongue jumped the track
    'Twixt the front and the back.
And got pinched in a bad anal spasm.

❧

Old Louis Quatorze was hot stuff.
He tired of that game, blindman's buff,
    Up-ended his mistress,
    Kissed hers while she kissed his,
And thus taught the world *soixante-neuf.*

There's a dowager near Sweden Landing
Whose manners are odd and demanding.
    It's one of her jests
    To suck off her guests–
She hates to keep gentlemen standing.

·

There was a young fellow named Taylor
Who seduced a respectable sailor.
    When they put him in jail
    He worked out the bail
By licking the parts of the jailer.

·

Have you heard of young Franchot Tone,
Who felt of his own peculiar bone?
    It was long and quite narrow
    And filled full of marrow,
And less edible than stale corn pone.

·

There was an old lady of Troy
Who invented a new kind of joy:
    She sugared her quim,
    And frosted the rim,
And then had it sucked by a boy.

A young man who lived in Balbriggan
Went to sea to recover from frigging,
    But after a week
    As they climbed the fore-peak
He buggered the mate in the rigging.


❧


Some night when you're drunk on Dutch Bols
Try changing the usual rôles.
    The backward position
    Is nice for coition
And it offers the choice of two holes.


❧


There was a young man from Chubut
Who had a remarkable root:
    When hard it would bend
    With a curve at the end,
So he fucked himself in the petoot.


❧


When she wanted a new way to futter
He greased her behind with butter;
    Then, with a sock,
    In went his jock,
And they carried her home on a shutter.

A Sultan of old Istamboul
Had a varicose vein in his tool.
   This evoked joyous grunts
    From his harem of cunts,
But his boys suffered pain at the stool.

There was a young fellow named Kelly
Who preferred his wife's ass to her belly.
   He shrieked with delight
    As he ploughed through the shite,
And filled up her hole with his jelly.

There was a young mate of a lugger
Who took out a girl just to hug her.
   "I've my monthlies," she said,
    "And a cold in the head,
But my bowels work well . . . Do you bugger?"

There was a young lady whose mind
Was never especially refined.
   She got on her knees,
    Her lover to please,
Who stuck in his prick from behind.

There was a young man from Nantasket
Who screwed a dead whore in a casket.
    He allowed 'twas no vice,
    But thought it was nice,
For she needed no money, nor'd ask it.

&#10087;

A phenomenal fellow named Preston
Has a hair-padded lower intestine.
    Though exceedingly fine
    In the buggery line,
It isn't much good for digestin'.

&#10087;

A modern monk nicknamed Augustin,
His penis a boy's bottom thrust in.
    Then said Father Ignatius,
    "Now really! Good gracious!
Your conduct is really disgusting."

&#10087;

There was a young Bishop from Brest
Who openly practiced incest.
    "My sisters and nieces
    Are all dandy pieces,
And they don't cost a cent," he confessed.

I once had the wife of a Dean
Seven times while the Dean was out ski'in'.
    She remarked with some gaiety,
    "Not bad for the laity,
Though the Bishop once managed thirteen."


There was a young monk from Dundee
Who hung a nun's cunt on a tree.
    He grabbed her fair ass
    And performed a high mass
That even the Pope came to see.


A rooster residing in Spain
Used to diddle his hens in the rain.
    "I give them a bloody
    Good time when it's muddy:
Which keeps them from getting too vain."


There was a young lady named Sutton
Who said, as she carved up the mutton,
    "My father preferred
    The last sheep in the herd—
This is one of his children I'm cuttin'."

There was a young lady of Wohl's Hill
Who sat herself down on a mole's hill.
   The resident mole
   Stuck his head up her hole—
The lady's all right, but the mole's ill.


ॐ


There was a young man of Bhogat,
The cheeks of whose ass were so fat
   That they had to be parted
   Whenever he farted,
And propped wide apart when he shat.


ॐ


There was a young lady of Dexter
Whose husband exceedingly vexed her,
   For whenever they'd start
   He'd unfailingly fart
With a blast that damn nearly unsexed her.


ॐ


There was a young woman named Dottie
Who said as she sat on her potty,
   "It isn't polite
   To do this in sight,
But then, who am I to be snotty?"

There was a young fellow of Ealing,
Devoid of all delicate feeling.
　　When he read on the door:
　　"Don't shit on the floor"
He jumped up and shat on the ceiling.

❧

There was a young virgin of Bude
Whose tricks, thought exciting, were viewed
　　With distrust by the males
　　For she'd fondle their rails,
But never would let them intrude.

❧

There was an old spinster named Campbell
Got tangled one day in a bramble.
　　She cried, "Ouch, how it sticks!
　　But so many sharp pricks
Are not met every day on a ramble."

❧

There was a young virgin of Dover
Who was raped in the woods by a drover.
　　When the going got hard
　　He greased her with lard,
Which felt nice, so they started all over.

There was a bluestocking in Florence
Wrote anti-sex pamphlets in torrents,
    Till a Spanish grandee
    Got her off with his knee,
And she burned all her works with abhorrence.


ਵ


A neuropath-virgin named Flynn
Shouted before she gave in:
    "It isn't the deed,
    Or the fear of the seed,
But that big worm that's shedding its skin!"


ਵ


There were three young ladies of Grimsby
Who said, "Of what use can our quims be?
    The hole in the middle
    Is so we can piddle,
But for what can the hole in the rims be?"


ਵ


There was a young girl from Hoboken
Who claimed that her hymen was broken
    From riding a bike
    On a cobblestone pike,
But it really was broken from pokin'.

A lady of virginal humours
Would only be screwed through her bloomers.
   But one fatal day
   The bloomers gave way,
Which fixed her for future consumers.

&#672;

No one can tell about Myrtle
Whether she's sterile or fertile.
   If anyone tries
   To tickle her thighs
She closes them tight like a turtle.

&#672;

A Newfoundland lad from Placentia
Was in love to the point of dementia,
   But his love couldn't burgeon
   With his touch-me-not virgin
'Til he screwed her by hand in absentia.

&#672;

There was a young lady from 'Quoddie
Who had a magnificent body,
   And her face was not bad,
   Yet she's never been had
For her odor was markèdly coddy.

A pathetic appellant at Reno
Was as chaste as the holy Bambino,
For she'd married a slicker
Who stuck to his liquor
And scorned her ripe maraschino.

❧

There was an old spinster of Tyre
Who bellowed, "My cunt is on fire!"
So a fireman was found,
Brought his engine around,
And extinguished her burning desire.

❧

There was a young lady of Worcester
Who dreamt that a rooster seduced her.
She woke with a scream,
But 'twas only a dream—
A bump in the mattress had goosed her.

❧

There was a young lady of France
Who went to the Palace to dance.
She danced with a Turk
Till he got in his dirk,
And now she can't button her pants.

A medical student named Hetrick
Is learnèd in matters obstetric.
   From a glance at the toes
   Of the mother, he knows
If the fetus's balls are symmetric.


&#672;


There was a young lady of Maine
Who declared she'd a man on the brain.
   But you knew from the view
   Of the way her waist grew,
It was not on her brain that he'd lain.


&#672;


There was an old whore of Marseilles
Who tried the new rotary spray.
   Said she, "Ah, that's better . . .
   Why here's a French letter
That's been missing since Armistice Day!"


&#672;


There was an old whore of Algiers
Who had bushels of dirt in her ears.
   The tip of her titty
   Was also quite shitty.
She never had washed it in years.

A young man, quite free with his dong,
Said the thing could be had for a song.
    Such response did he get
    That he rented the Met,
And held auditions all the day long.

❧

A sempstress at Epping-on-Tyne
 Used to peddle her tail down the line.
    She first got a crown,
    But her prices went down—
Now she'll fit you for ten pence or nine.

❧

There was a young lady of Erskine,
And the chief of her charms was her fair skin,
    But the sable she wore
    (She had several more)
She had earned while wearing her bare skin.

❧

A shiftless young fellow of Kent
Had his wife fuck the landlord for rent.
    But as she grew older
    The landlord grew colder,
And now they live out in a tent.

Any whore whose door sports a red light
Knows a prick when she sees one, all right.
   She can tell by a glance
   At the drape of men's pants
If they're worth taking on for the night.

ॐ

There was a young lady named Mable
Who would fuck on a bed or a table.
   Though a two-dollar screw
   Was the best she could do,
Her ass bore a ten-dollar label.

ॐ

Said a naked young soldier named Mickey
As his cunt eyed his stiff, throbbing dickey,
   "Kid, my leave's almost up,
   But I feel like a tup;
Bend down, and I'll slip you a quickie."

ॐ

A school marm from old Mississippi
Had a quim that was simply zippy.
   The scholars all praised it
   Till finally she raised it
To prices befitting a chippy.

There was a young thing from Missouri
Who fancied herself as a houri.
   Her friends thus forsook her,
   For a harlot they took her,
And she gave up the role in a fury.

     ❧

There was a young lady named Moore
Who, while not quite precisely a whore,
   Couldn't pass up a chance
   To take down her pants,
And compare some man's stroke with her bore.

     ❧

A tired young trollop of Nome
Was worn out from her toes to her dome.
   Eight miners came screwing,
   But she said, "Nothing doing;
*One* of you has to go home!"

     ❧

A chippy whose name was O'Dare
Sailed on a ship to Kenmare,
   But this cute little honey
   Had left home her money
So she laid the whole crew for her fare.

Says a busy young whore named Miss Randalls,
As men by the dozens she handles,
   "When I get this busy
   My cunt gets all jizzy,
And it runs down my legs like wax candles."


There was a young lady in Reno
Who lost all her dough playing keeno.
   But she lay on her back
   And opened her crack,
And now she owns the casino.


There was an old girl of Silesia
Who said, "As my cunt doesn't please ya,
   You might as well come
   Up my slimy old bum,
But be careful my tapeworm don't seize ya."


There was a young whore from Tashkent
Who managed an immoral tent.
   Day out and day in
   She lay writhing in sin,
Giving thanks it was ten months to Lent.

There once was a knowledgeful whore
Who knew all the coital lore.
    But she found there were many
    Who preferred her fat fanny,
And now she don't fuck any more.


There once was a versatile whore,
As expert behind as before.
    For a quid you could view her,
    And bugger and screw her,
As she stood on her head on the floor.


There was a young fellow—a banker,
Had bubo, itch, pox, and chancre.
    He got all the four
    From the dirty old whore,
So he wrote her a letter to thank her.


There was a young man of Back Bay
Who thought syphilis just went away,
    And felt that a chancre
    Was merely a canker
Acquired in lascivious play.

There was an old man of Goditch,
Had the syph and the clap and the itch.
   His name was McNabs
   And he also had crabs,
The dirty old son of a bitch.

❦

An explorer returned from Australia,
Reported lost paraphernalia:
   A Zeiss microscope
   And his personal hope,
Which had vanished with his genitalia.

❦

There was an old maid from Bermuda
Who shot a marauding intruder.
   It was not her ire
   At his lack of attire,
But he reached for her jewels as he screwed her.

❦

A miner who bored in Brazil
Found some very strange rust on his drill.
   He thought it a joke
   Till the bloody thing broke—
Now his tailings are practically nil.

An eccentric young poet named Brown
Raised up his embroidered gown
   To look for his peter
   To beat it to metre,
But fainted when none could be found.


The wife of a red-headed Celt
Lost the key to her chastity-belt.
   She tried picking the lock
   With an Ulsterman's cock,
And the next thing he knew, he was gelt.


The wife of an athlete named Chuck
Found her married life shit-out-of-luck.
   Her husband played hockey
   Without wearing a jockey—
Now he hasn't got what it takes for a fuck.


There was a young girl from the Creek
Who had her periods twice every week.
   "How very provoking,"
   Said the Vicar from Woling,
"There's no time for poking, so to speak."

The wife of a chronic crusader
Took on every man who waylaid her.
   Till the amorous itch
   Of this popular bitch
So annoyed the crusader he spayed her.


&#x2767;


There was a young fellow named Nick
Who was cursed with a spiralling prick.
   So he set out to hunt
   For a screw-twisted cunt
That would match with his corkscrewy dick.


He found one, and took it to bed,
And then in chagrin he dropped dead,
   For that spiralling snatch
   It never would match—
The damn thing had a left-handed thread!


&#x2767;


A gallant young Frenchman named Grandhomme
Was attempting a girl on a tandem.
   At the height of the make
   She slammed on the brake,
And scattered his semen at random.

There was an old sheik named Al Hassid
Whose tool had become very placid.
   Before each injection
   To get an erection
He had to immerse it in acid.

&#2766;

Said old Mr. Wellington Koo,
"Now what in the Hell shall I do?
   My wife is too hot,
   I can't fill up her slot—"
So he screwed her to bits trying to.

&#2766;

A crooner who lived in Lahore
Got his balls caught in a door.
   Now his mezzo soprano
   Is rather piano
Though he was a loud basso before.

&#2766;

There was a young man of Bagdad
Who was dreaming that he was a shad.
   He dreamt he was spawning,
   And then, the next morning,
He found that, by Jesus! he had.

An eunuch frequenting Bangkok
Used to borrow the deified jock
   From a local rain-god
   When he went for a prod—
You could hear the girl yell for a block.

&#x2767;

There was a young naval cadet
Whose dreams were unusually wet.
   When he dreamt of his wedding
   He soaked up the bedding,
And the wedding ain't taken place yet.

&#x2767;

There was a gay Countess of Dufferin,
One night while her husband was covering,
   Just to chaff him a bit
   She said, "You old shit,
I can buy a dildo for a sovereign."

&#x2767;

As Apollo was chasing the fair
Daphne she vanished in air.
   He could find but a shrub
   With thick bark on the hub
And not even a knot-hole to spare.

There were three young ladies of Fetters,
Annoyed all their elders and betters
    By stuffing their cock-holders
    With proxies for stockholders,
Old bills, and anonymous letters.

There was a young parson of Goring
Who made a small hole in the flooring.
    He lined it all round,
    Then laid on the ground,
And declared it was cheaper than whoring.

A vicious old whore of Albania
Hated men with a terrible mania.
    With a twitch and a squirm
    She would hold back your sperm,
And then roll on her face and disdain ya.

There was a young man of Kutki
Who could blink himself off with one eye.
    For a while though, he pined,
    When his organ declined
To function, because of a stye.

An innocent boy in Lapland
Was told that frigging was grand.
    But at his first trial
    He said with a smile,
"I've had the same feeling by hand."

There is a young fellow from Leeds
Whose skin is so thin his cock bleeds
    Whenever erect;
    This dermal defect
Often scares him from sowing his seeds.

There was a young fellow from Lees
Who handled his tool with great ease.
    This continual friction
    Made his sex a mere fiction,
But the callus hangs down to his knees.

There was a young man from McGill
Who was always seen walking uphill.
    When someone inquired,
    "My man, aren't you tired?"
He said, "No, it makes my balls thrill."

There was a young man named M'Gurk
Who dozed off one night after work.
　　He had a wet dream
　　But awoke with a scream
Just in time to give it a jerk.


❧


There was a young lady named May
Who frigged herself in the hay.
　　She bought a pickle—
　　One for a nickel—
And wore all the warts away!


❧


A nymphomaniacal nurse
With a curse that was worse than perverse
　　Stuck a rotary drill
　　Up her twat, for a thrill—
And they carted her off in a hearse.


❧


A eunuch who came from Port Said
Had a jolly good time in bed,
　　Nor could any sultana
　　Detect from his manner
That he used a banana instead.

A reformer who went out to Bali
To change the sartorial folly
　　Of the girls now admits,
　　"A pair of good tits
In season can seem rather jolly."

　　　　❧

There was a young Queen of Baroda
Who built a new kind of pagoda.
　　The walls of its halls
　　Were festooned with the balls
And the tools of the fools that bestrode her.

　　　　❧

There was a young lady in Brent,
When her old man's pecker it bent,
　　She said with a sigh,
　　"Oh, why must it die?
Let's fill it with Portland Cement."

　　　　❧

There was an old man from Bubungi
Whose balls were all covered with fungi.
　　With his friends, out at lunch,
　　He tore off a bunch
And said, "Now divide this among ye."

A mystical painter named Foxx
Once picked up a girl on the docks.
    He made an elliptic
    Mysterious triptych,
And painted it right on her box.


&#42;


There was a young cowboy named Gary
Who was morbidly anxious to marry,
    But he found the defection
    Of any erection
A difficult factor to parry.


&#42;


A young baseball-fan named Miss Glend
Was the home-team's best rooter and friend.
    But for her the big league
    Never held the intrigue
Of a bat with two balls at the end.


&#42;


The favorite pastime of grandfather
Was tickling his balls with a feather.
    But the thing he liked best
    Of all the rest
Was knocking them gently together.

There was a young man named Ignatius
Who lived in a garret quite spacious.
    When he went to his auntie's
    He always wore panties,
But alone in his garret—good gracious!

&#10087;

There is a young nurse in Japan
Who lifts men by their pricks to the pan.
    A trick of jujitsu,
    And either it shits you
Or makes you feel more like a man.

&#10087;

The prick of a young man of Kew
Showed veins that were azure of hue.
    Its head was quite red
    So he waved it and said,
"Three cheers for the red, white, and blue."

&#10087;

A clever inventory named Krupp
Wore a belt when he wanted to tup.
    His mighty dry cells
    Made her tits buzz like bells,
And lighted the hall-entrance up.

Quoth the coroner's jury in Preston,
"The verdict is rectal congestion."
    They found an eight-ball
    On a shoemaker's awl
Halfway up the major's intestine.

❧

There was a young lady of Asia
Who had an odd kind of aphasia.
    She'd forget that her cunt
    Was located in front,
Which deprived her of most of the pleasure.

❧

There was a young girl of Asturias
With a penchant for practices curious.
    She loved to bat rocks
    With her gentlemen's cocks—
A practice both rude and injurious.

❧

A lecherous fellow named Babbitt
Asked a girl if she'd fuck or would nab it.
    Said she, "From long habit
    I fuck like a rabbit,
So I'd rather cohabit than grab it."

The ancient orthographer, Chisholm,
Caused a lexicographical schism
    When he asked to know whether
    'Twere known which was better
To use—*g* or *j*—to spell *jism*.

&#x2767;

The Duchess of Drood's lewd and crude,
And the men think her terribly rude.
    When they swim by the docks
    She tickles their cocks
And laughs when the red tips protrude.

&#x2767;

A certain young lady named Daisy
Who is really infernally lazy
    Said, "I haven't the time
    To wipe my behine,
But the way I can hump drives 'em crazy."

&#x2767;

A surly and pessimist Druid,
A defeatist, if only he knew it,
    Said, "The world's on the skids,
    And I think having kids
Is a waste of good seminal fluid."

A company of Grenadier Guards
While traversing the park, formed in squads,
    Saw two naked statues
    At three-quarter pratt views,
Which perceptibly stiffened their rods.

There was a young athlete named Grimmon
Who developed a new way of swimmin':
    By a marvellous trick
    He would scull with his prick,
Which attracted loud cheers from the women.

There once was a lady hand-letterer
Who thought of a program to better her.
    She hand-lettered each
    Of the parts she could reach,
The bosoms, the navel, et cetera.

An ingenious young fellow named Herman
Tied a bow on the end of his worm, and
    His wife said, "How festive!"
    But he said, "Don't be restive—
You'll wriggle it off with your squirmin'."

When Angelico worked in cerise,
For the angel he painted his niece.
   In a heavenly trance
   He pulled off her pants,
And erected a fine altar-piece.


❧


A mason, one of the Malones
 Put a coat of cement on his stones.
   "They keep warmer at night,
   And are bound to hang tight,
And not bruise themselves on my knee-bones."


❧


There was an eccentric from Mecca
Who discovered a record from Decca,
   Which he twirled on his thumb
   (Those eccentrics are dumb)
While he needled the disc with his pecca.


❧


A musicienne in gay Montebello
Amused herself playing the cello,
   But not a solo,
   For she used as a bow
The dong of a sturdy young fellow.

A bather whose clothing was strewed
By the winds that left her quite nude,
 Saw a man come along,
 And unless we are wrong
You expected this line to be lewd.


&#8227;


The dong of a fellow named Grable
Was as pliant and long as a cable.
 Each night while he ate,
 This confirmed reprobate
Would screw his wife under the table.


&#8227;


There was a young man from Peru
Whose lineage was noble all through.
 Now this isn't crud,
 For not only his blood
But even his semen was blue.


&#8227;


There was a young man from Saskatchewan
Whose pecker was truly gargantuan.
 It was good for large whores
 And small dinosaurs,
And sufficiently rough to scratch a match upon.

There was a young man named Murray
Who made love to his girl in a surrey.
   She started to sigh
   But someone walked by,
So he buttoned his pants in a hurry.

       ❧

A young man whose sight was myopic
Thought sex an incredible topic.
   So poor were his eyes,
   That despite its great size,
His penis appeared microscopic.

       ❧

There was a young man named O'Neill,
Used to play on the old Campanile.
   He made the gong bong
   With the end of his dong—
Now he's trying to get it to heal.

       ❧

A prudish young damsel named Rose
Is particular how men propose.
   To "Let's have intercourse,"
   She says gaily, "Of course,"
But to "Let's fuck," she turns up her nose.

Said a certain sweet red-headed siren,
"Young sailors are cute—I must try one!"
   She came home in the nude,
   Stewed, screwed, and tattooed
With lewd pictures and verses from Byron.

     ❧

There was a young man up in Utah
Who constructed a cundum of pewter.
   He said, "I confess
   You feel nothing or less,
But it makes you as safe as a neuter."

     ❧

A fanatic gun-lover named Crust
Was perverse to the point of disgust.
   His idea of a peach
   Had a sixteen-inch breech,
And a pearl-handled 44 bust.

     ❧

A daring young maid from Dubuque
Risked a rather decided rebuke
   By receiving a prude
   In the absolute nude,
But he gasped, "IF you only could cook!"

If Leo your own birthday marks
You will fuck until 40, when starts
   A new pleasure in stamps,
   Boy Scouts and their camps,
And fondling nude statues in parks.


There was a young blade from South Greece
Whose bush did so greatly increase
   That before he could shack
   He must hunt needle in stack.
'Twas as bad as being obese.


There once was a gay young Parisian
Who screwed an appendix incision,
   And the girl of his choice
   Could hardly rejoice
At this horrible lack of precision.


There once was a cuntlapper's daughter
Who, despite all her father had taught her,
   Would become so unstrung
   At the touch of a tongue
That she'd deluge her beau with her water.